FAT GIRL MAGIC

KAT SAVAGE

central
avenue
POETRY

2024

Published by Central Avenue Poetry, an imprint of Central Avenue Marketing Ltd.
www.centralavenuepublishing.com

FAT GIRL MAGIC

978-1-77168-362-3 (pbk)
978-1-77168-363-0 (ebk)

Published in Canada
Printed in United States of America

1. POETRY / Women Authors   2. POETRY / Subject & Themes - General

1 3 5 7 9 1 8 6 4 2

Keep up with Central Avenue

For my mother,
who told me I could be anything I wanted.
I did it, Mama.

TRIGGER WARNING

Some of the poems contained in this collection mention
body image and diet culture, and allude to eating
disorders and negative viewpoints of fatness, though
this is only intended to paint an accurate picture
of what is experienced living in a fat body. Some of
the poems contained in this collection also contain
terminology associated with witchcraft and spellwork.

A SPELL FOR THE HURT

add precisely fourteen insults you were given
before you turned eighteen into a bowl,
and break your hand mixing them into
something that resembles snake oil

add to this mixture one pound of flesh
because everyone wants a piece of you
and you don't know how to say no

when it reaches a syrup-like consistency,
add lavender

always add lavender
to everything,
the good and bad

if you have any broken promises
lying around, chop them up and
add a few pinches or a whole bowl,
whatever feels right

light a blood-red candle at your altar

repeat three times:
this is what I deserve,
I know no other way than this

drink it up like it's your only option
but don't be alarmed if it tastes like sweat
or piss or worse: regret—you'll get used to it

we all get used to it

welcome to the coven

what is this hold the mirror has on me?

why do I let it make me cry?

is it too late to cover them all up

and pretend I don't know what I look like?

is it too late to stop hating myself for existing?

THE LOSS OF WEIGHT AND OTHER THINGS

This year, coupled with the one before it, has made me fat. Or rather, fatter. I stand in front of one of those cruel full-length mirrors and pinch at rolls I didn't have a few years ago. I grimace. I don't understand how men touch me, let alone fuck me.

I don't eat anything after two p.m. Over the whole day, I only eat four things. Not four meals. Four individual things. And that's two more than I wanted to eat. I know what's happening. It always goes like this. I start to hate my body again and it knows. I lose my appetite without realizing it.

My body begins to shrink faster than it should. I don't notice until one day my clothes are sagging and I get to rip into my bottom drawer. The one filled with all my *skinny clothes*.

I touch my body again in front of the mirror and I know it's smaller, but I can't see it. I'm still too big. Always too big. So I eat less. Until one day, I try on the pair of jeans held on to for the past five years with a desperate need to be able to wear them again.

They fit.
And I'm happy.
My eyes and cheeks are sunken in, but I'm smiling.

What a shame.

TINDER MOMENTS #1

you told me you prefer
your women more petite
and told me to have a good day

then you blocked me
before I could respond

I didn't even get to tell you
to have a good day too

ACCORDING TO THE CHURCH

for Trish from California

they'll never say it out loud,
it'll never be more than what you can
read between the lines as they whisper it
over the offering plate

and even then, they've never been better
at playing a game of denial as you take
communion and slip on your purity ring

cleanliness is not the thing next to godliness,
unless you mean your bedpost

prettiness, thinness, obedience—
those are the marks of a godly woman
in the eyes of an institution
I had to say goodbye to
just to survive

FUNNY FAT FRIEND

(insert comic relief) because I know the title makes you shift in your seat, a discomfort similar to wool fabric against the skin

(insert self-deprecating joke) because it's easier to point at myself and laugh than wait for you and your group of friends to beat me to the punch

(insert comic relief) from just outside the frame, spotlight to the left of me, everyone happy, smiling, in love while I stand in the shadows and wait for the next place I can interject something about myself to laugh at

(insert another self-deprecating joke) because I don't know who I am without them, because I'm not the leading lady and if I list out the reasons why I can't be, like they're something to laugh at, it won't hurt as much

CONTROL THE CURVE
for Samantha from California

not fair, not fair, not fair

the girl to your right eyes your body,
grows green with jealousy, chants

not fair, not fair, not fair

tells you a white girl shouldn't have a big butt,
like you pulled it from a department store rack,
like you paid extra for it

she laughs to mask her hatred for your body,
that her body isn't like your body

not fair, not fair, not fair

there are two victims here,
two girls learning
their flesh will be judged

the chanter goes on,
forgets, laughs it off,
no big deal

but you hold on to this moment,
let it cling to you like a wild animal
grips its mother,
feel it each time you look at

your backside in a mirror,

remember her scowl and think,

not fair, not fair, not fair

I didn't do anything to deserve this,
I didn't ask for any of this

Is there a petition to make women's pants sizes measure
like men's pants sizes with real—not arbitrary—numbers,
or are we failing?

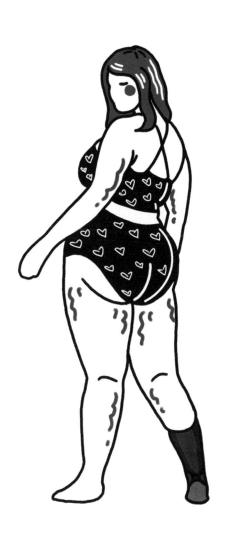

TINDER MOMENTS #2

he told me
he'd always wanted to
fuck a fat chick,
asked me if I wanted
to fulfill that fantasy

I almost said yes

and that makes me so sad

POUND OF FLESH

for Georgana from South Carolina

they wanted theirs,
their pound of flesh,
wanted to make a sideshow out of me
under the watchful eyes of those who have
not yet lived enough life to judge others

pound of flesh, pound of flesh

I still hear their sneers late at night
when I think about it a moment too long,
their petty laughs as they pointed at the scale,
untamed and uncaring adolescence

pound of flesh, pound of flesh

but they didn't break me—
I didn't let them see my tears,
my shame, my reddened cheeks

they won't get my dignity from me

pound of flesh, pound of flesh

did they consider the price?

DIET. CULTURE.

16 points.
1,327 calories.
12 grams of protein.
53 carbohydrates.
4 servings of vegetables.
0 salt.

I write it all down with a precision I haven't indulged since
eleventh-grade advanced chemistry.
I went over my calorie count today so I need to do
250 EXTRA sit-ups before bed.

drink 200 ounces of water.
20 minutes of cardio.
6-minute stretch.

add. subtract. sacrifice.

on Friday, I get to treat myself to 3 cookies.

next week, I'll start fasting.
4 hours of eating.
20 hours of water.
juice if I feel faint.
acetaminophen for the headaches.

it'll be worth it.

when the scale dips lower, lower again,
I can start my meal replacement shakes.

it'll be worth it.

EVERYDAY BATTLE

for Anonymous from Louisiana

Biggie

       Biggie

              Biggie

that's what the other kids called me,
just one of the weapons they wielded
to rip my soul apart,
ignorant of the lifelong damage
they were causing

Biggie

       Biggie

              Biggie

plays on the radio in the car
and I'm not a grown woman anymore,
I'm back in eighth grade, sobbing and panicking,
sobbing some more

and so an endless cycle
of self-destruction plays on—
the comfort and addiction
of food, of the one thing
I drown in

so none of us need your
constant reminders

we know we're fat

202/SOS

I am rounded belly
and thick thighs

there is an X on the tags
of my clothing,
and the bathroom scale
reads 202

if I stare at it long enough,
my vision blurs,
my eyes begin to water,
and it looks like
SOS

men say to me
you are too big,
you'd be prettier if you lost weight,
I prefer petite women
but you've got a nice face

I don't have time
for conditional love,
and the only thing
heavy here is how
their words weigh me down,
anchor to my skin,
latch on to me
like locks of condemnation

I am sinking to the bottom of the river,
and they took the keys with them
when they left

ELEVEN
for Tiff from Washington

the first time someone called me fat,
I was eleven years old,
standing on the precipice of womanhood,
still mostly child

which is to say,
I was still a baby growing into myself,
still half-cocoon, very nearly still
soft-boned, definitely all soft-hearted,
a new bud on a twig

it's been more than two decades
and still it grips me,
still it makes me hold my head down
in the mirror now and again,
still the wound aches

which is to say,
you should be careful what you say,
careful you don't harden that which is still soft,
careful what you speak into existence

A FAT GIRL GOES GROCERY SHOPPING UNDER A CLOAK OF SHAME AS IF HER FATNESS MEANS SHE SHOULD NOT EAT

I'm standing in front of a cooler of boneless skinless chicken breasts and working out the math in my head. How many do I need to eat in order to be considered *healthy*? How many will absolve me from my social sins? The eyes of strangers burn into my backside. I feel their judgment for every item in my cart. I hide the peanut butter cups under a bag of spinach. And later when I eat them, I'll feel a special sort of twofold shame. *I had to hide these. I had to eat them alone.* Who knew peanut butter cups could be so controversial. I grab an extra pack of the boneless skinless chicken breasts and head to the next aisle in search of the zero fat, zero sugar, plain Greek yogurt to assuage my guilt.

I press my body into the mattress, hoping like hell it will swallow some or all of me. I wonder how small I can make myself look or feel. If I don't let my hands memorize the lines of my body, they won't know I'm more sphere, swollen. If I remain in the dark, cover all the mirrors, remain unmoved . . . *maybe*. I pull my knees to my chest, tuck my feet in, cloak myself in heavy blankets. The only thing still in sight is my pretty face. My face *too pretty for a fat body*, they say. I don't know what to do with that kind of backhanded compliment so I tuck it deep into my pocket and only bring it out on special occasions. But here's what I know to be true. Other people try to rationalize to themselves why I'm fat more than I try to rationalize it to myself.

I

am

always

too

much

of

something

and

somehow

never

enough

NO LOVE. ALL INHERITANCE

for Christina from California

my husband needed meat,
more than I had, but I'd just given life from my body,
so he cheated because I was bone
and he needed meat,
needed me to be more,
so I left him

years later, I gave my love
to another man, but now I had too much meat
and he wanted more bone,
asked me to stick to salads,
asked me to be less,
so we were doomed too

my mother pinches the rolls at my waistline,
calls it a *muffin top*,
does it just to remind me it exists,
to remind me I'm not free from it

all the women of my family
embrace and pass on
their unhealthy obsessions
with weight,
with body image,
an inheritance I never asked for,
one I hope I can escape

MOTHER'S MILK

my mother gave me two things:

life

and

an awareness—no, a hatred—
for my own body

little girls do
        as mothers do

we comb our hair,
put on lipstick,
and we pinch our thighs

they're jealous when
we're smaller than them,
revel in our fatness when
we grow larger than them,
remind us with their words,
their eyes,

how we ended up exactly like them

it's all we wanted as little girls,
to be just like them

little did we know it came with a tax

I never saw a fat princess growing up. They were never curvy, never something thick. Always petite. Always, as the kids say, *snatched waist*. Even cartoon girls bound themselves in corsets. It was always the villain, always the evil stepsister, stepmother, ugly witch with chubby bellies and double chins. What kind of woman did they expect me to grow up to be when I only ever saw myself in the face of the wicked?

SUCH GOOD LIARS

I should like to go
to the tall green grass

and sit
and sigh

and feel something
beyond this cage
I've put myself in

to feel free
of this brokenness
I carry

because I know nothing else,
because I believe I can be
nothing else

society beats this into me,
the women on the billboards,
the men in the streets,

they are such good liars

and I have been fed their bitterness for so long
I don't know what lies beyond it

what is the cage? what is freedom?

Last night in my dream, I was thin. Not very thin. I want to be clear about this fact. But a noticeable difference when compared to my reality. So while I attempt every single day to be happy and satisfied in my own skin, in this body I am learning to love, there's still a part of me deep down in my subconscious, or whatever part of my brain controls dreaming, that's already bowed to the universal expectation. There's a part of me that betrays the rest every night as I sleep. And the sadness runneth over.

IF YOU STAY

if you stay,
I'll bake you banana bread and serve it to you
with chamomile from my window box garden

if you stay,
I'll let you do that thing in bed you keep asking me
to do even though I already said no

if you stay,
I'll go to the gym every day and drink water
and always do my makeup so I don't embarrass you

if you stay,
you can pick every TV show, and I promise to always
know where I want to eat when you ask me

if you stay,
I'll never ask you to put down the toilet seat
or pick up your towel ever again

if you stay,
I'll lose as much weight as you want and never
say a word when you check out skinnier girls

if you stay,
I promise I can make you happy this time and
you won't want to cheat again

if you stay,
I promise I won't throw this in your face in our
next fight and I'll forget it ever happened

if you stay,
I'll give you babies and blow jobs and a wholehearted
promise I'll never ask you to go again

what I mean is, if you stay,
I'll forget my own identity and strip away my boundary lines,
forget your indiscretions, and anything else, to keep your love

TRAIN WRECK

I am good enough to look at
but not good enough to touch

I am good enough to look at
but not good enough to touch

I am a train wreck you pass
impossibly slowly—
you're unable to look away from
my billowing black smoke and shrapnel
flying through the air like startled birds
and home run baseballs

in so many ways
you think I'm beautiful,
and in so many ways
you are relieved to be
at a safe distance

you cannot look away
from my magnificence,
but you're so glad
you're not mangled in my steel

I am good enough to look at
but not good enough to touch

I am good enough to look at
but not good enough to touch

because what would everyone think?

Sometimes I don't wipe the fog from the mirrors when I get out of the shower. It's easier to look at my body when it's distorted behind a streaked curtain. I pat my skin dry as quickly as I can because I'm standing naked and know my lover wouldn't think twice about walking in. My heart races against itself as I race against time to cover myself before he can open the door and uncover me. I like to forget he's seen me before. Forget he's touched my body with love and heat and acceptance. I can hardly stand the thought of looking at myself. I don't know how he stomachs it. The doorknob begins to click as I rush to wrap my body into a cold, damp towel. The knob clicks a second time and I realize I remembered to lock it. Saved myself again.

GHOST FAT

It's gone but I still see it
each time I find myself
in front of a reflective surface

a glass door,
the side of my car,
sometimes even the convex of a spoon

wrinkled clothes resembling
not-quite-forgotten rolls,
a body that still looks just as thick
as it did before

it's gone but I can still feel it
each time I run my hands
over my naked skin,
body smaller than before
and yet my fingertips
search for it, convinced
of its existence

it's gone but I know it's still here,
I know everyone can still see it,
know they're still passing silent judgments

it's gone but it's never really gone

I'm surrounded by people
telling me anyone would
be lucky to have me
and yet no one
is touching me

everyone wants a hug
but no one is embracing me

this is the lonely side
of a sleepless night

UPHILL

for Bri from Oregon

he whispers words
of love into my skin,
into my heart,
speaks of perfection, of beauty
and unconditional adoration

I find it all so hard to believe,
such big pills to swallow,
words I can't quite let myself accept

my hands feel for every flaw,
magnified by generational scars,
words cut into my flesh long ago

I trudge uphill
over and over again
like the man doomed
to roll a rock

I trudge,
I try,
I try again

A SPELL FOR THE HOPE

if you've made it this far, congratulations,
this is intermediate spellwork and can be tricky business
but if you pay close attention, you'll make it through

there are three or four pivotal moments
when you realize you need more than
what you've been accepting
add all of them to a bowl and mull it into powder

you need a dead man's voice box,
one you cut out with your own bravery
yours hasn't been working and you're going to need
to start speaking up
yell if you must

ignite a stick of palo santo or sage (but not white),
either will work, and cleanse your body of all the negative
things you say about it

remove all the words that have been thrown at it
until you find yourself a blank canvas once again

add lavender to your voice box powder,
a scoop of nettle leaf for courage,
sprinkle in chamomile for wisdom
and a heavy-handed pour of cinnamon for happiness

repeat three times:
*grant me the strength to use my voice,
to protect my body, to find hope*

add mixture to a hot bath and soak yourself until you prune*

best if performed during a full moon but the moment you need it most will also work

SALT CIRCLES

how do I protect myself
from the darkness
when everything tells me
I was born to it

I'm scared to know what happens
when I break the salt circle
around my heart

I'm scared to know what happens
when my toes kick up the edge of the one
surrounding my bed

do my bones know
they're good now,
or have I failed my body
for too long—
have I left it unprepared
for the words strangers will say about it?

when I was a baby,
I lay in a dresser drawer pulled
from my eighteen-year-old mother's chest,
a makeshift crib in her grandfather's house,
a baby raising a baby

she didn't know then
what I would become,
the woman I would grow to be

(I didn't know either)

she didn't know
she birthed the sickness
and the cure

I'm waiting for the day I don't need
salt circles,
but rather am a salt circle myself,
and stand beneath a great white oak,
inhale smoke
because I burned down
the hanging tree

if you speak of me
in some far-off time,
please let it be about the way
I always tried to heal
myself and others,
let it be for how
I never gave up

not even when I was
choking on table salt

not even when
I kneeled in broken glass,
cut my knees just to
resuscitate my blackened lungs

not even when I wanted
more than anything
to stop
to give up
to surrender
let them know I never did

Sometimes I dream I'm floating through a dark and cloudless sky, upward toward the cosmos. There are only a few visible stars freckling the great beyond, but none of that matters.

I am w e i g h t l e s s.

I don't feel my body, its heaviness, its burden. No one is laughing at me, no one is sneering.

I am f r e e.

For as long as I can manage, I bask in it, cling to it as it slips slowly through my fingertips, slowly as I sink back down toward my bed. I plead with the sandman to let me feel this a little longer, but he only smiles and waves as I pass him. My head hits the pillow, my body gently cradled back into my mattress. And then I'm awake.

I am t r a p p e d again.

showing my body
to the world
should not be considered
an act of bravery

WHAT I IMAGINE

for Daniele from California

when I'm alone,
I feel perfect in every way,
but surrounded by people,
an overwhelming feeling
of being less than,
of being not good enough,
takes over

my fantasies have
branded me beautiful,
but others don't see
the same in me

so what is real?
what am I to believe?

I slip deep into a sadness,
hoping one day I don't
feel so lonely anymore,
especially in the
presence of others

I fight,
I fight,
I say nothing,
but I fight

to ignore their words,
to one day love myself

FIXED IT

You're pretty ~~for a fat girl~~

You have a nice face ~~for someone your size~~

You are beautiful, ~~you should lose weight~~

You eat healthy ~~to be so fat~~

You're flexible ~~for someone your size~~

HOW YOU WEEP

Fat Girl,
how you weep,
tears falling from the altostratus—
nourishing salt
for the Earth

you wipe them away,
punish delicate cheeks
with rough touch,
pink and puffy,
a tainted cherub

a man used his words like weapons,
tried to beat you down with
a string of juvenile insults,
tried to make you bleed for him,
passive aggression seeping from
his snarling snout

Mother Queen,
you have given back to the Earth,
and he has given nothing,
he *is nothing*

one day he will beg you to let him taste you,
to spread your thick thighs for him,
but he'll ask you to keep your shirt on,
tell you to keep it a secret,
so you tell him you don't remember who he is,
you tell him *only kings can taste you*

it's only a half-lie,
because queens always remember,
always tuck away the moments
that shape us, and even though
we dig them up just to torture
ourselves from time to time,

at least now you know your worth

A PRISON OF BLACK

the orange jumpsuit
of plus-sized clothing
is the color black

black is slimming

if I wear black,
does that mean the cashier
won't see my fat?
is it a disappearing act?
an invisible cloak?

if I wear black,
does that mean the guy on Tinder
who likes my face
but hasn't seen my body
won't stare below my neck
on our first date
and wonder why a woman
with such a pretty face
has to be fat?

does it make me disappear into my
surroundings like camouflage?

no? I didn't think so

I guess whether I wear
the drab black number
or the bubblegum pink halter top
I'll be the same size

so I guess I should wear whatever
makes me happiest

I should wear whatever
the hell I want

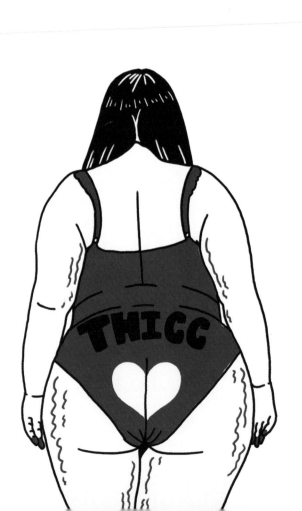

I grow tired of pretending my fat is the only thing worthy of writing about or defending, or whatever you want to call it. As if I don't have a hundred other beautiful parts I could write about. People act like no one wants to hear the way the light hits my nebula eyes and I've had one or two men think they were astronauts. How a few of them died in the valley of my sternum, lost and looking for water. How I've been held in the darkness as I fell apart, slipping through fingertips. How I've been lost and found in the landscape of bedsheets. But no one wants to drown in the love of a fat girl. No one wants to hear the air leave our lungs.

THICK GIRL SWAY

thick girl,
pretty little thick girl
show me how you sway

thick girl slide
thick girl glide
thick girl sway

thick girl does what you want
thick girl learns to dance
thick girl gives good head
thick girl doesn't cry

thick girl,
sexy little thick girl
show me how you fuck

thick girl moan
thick girl groan
thick girl fuck

thick girl cooks for you
thick girl cleans for you
thick girl bakes for you
thick girl never complains to you

thick girl,
sad little thick girl
show me how you hide

thick girl cry
thick girl shy
thick girl hide

thick girl,
mad little thick girl
show me how you dream

thick girl leaves
thick girl lives
thick girl dreams

NOTHING ELSE MATTERS WHEN YOU'RE THIN & PRETTY

for Tasara from California

it's all people pay attention to—
is she thin?
is she pretty?

I existed as both,
sported them like badges of honor,
like something I earned
rather than the luck of the draw

I was sad, but that didn't matter—
I was thin and pretty
and so I could fold my sadness
into my back pocket, tuck it into my purse

I would say,
I'm so sad

and they'd say,
but you're thin and pretty

and then I'd say,
yeah, that's true

but now I'm fat—fat and tired and old and still sad,
except it doesn't fit in my pocket anymore

but people don't come to me and say,
I'm so sorry you're sad

no, instead they say,
I'm so sorry you're old and fat—

you wouldn't be so tired if you were skinny
because no one sees *me,*
not my sadness,
not my happiness,
not my art
or my love

they're blind to my laughter,
my tears,
my heart

all they can see is my body, my fat body
and they sigh, turn away

but that's okay

beneath my fat is a rib cage,
beneath my rib cage is a heart
and it beats
and it beats
and it beats
wildly,
wonderfully,
and full of hope

that one day the love I have for myself will be enough,
that one day I will be able to leave the sadness at home
for a little while

and the people, they'll say to me,
look how beautiful your soul is

look
how it shines

I am a fat girl

I am not a fetish

Do you think the price of a salad is eight dollars and the price of a cheeseburger is two dollars to intentionally create a gap between healthy living and the impoverished, or are you blind?

the Renaissance knew,
cherished our thickness,
saw fertility in the roundness
of our bellies,
immortalized us in oil paintings
and marble statues

now they want us to hide,
fold ourselves into the shadows,
cloak our bodies in thick layers,
erase us from the landscape of society

they wanna say we are nothing to praise,
nothing to adore,
nothing worth worship

but we know better than that
don't we, Goddess?

they are the only ones
who should feel shame

A STAYING-OR-GOING INCANTATION

I put you in a spell jar,
layered you on top of snow-white salt
from the Dead Sea

sprinkled rosemary on the crown of your head,
made you a blanket of lavender,
a pinch of sage under your scented pillow

loaded up your back with citrine and hematite,
tried to manifest you from nothing

your name is scrawled in ink on a tiny slip of paper,
repeated three times, rolled tight, bound in red thread,
thrown in flames

sprinkled in mugwort and yarrow for good measure,
inhaled the smoke so deeply I began to choke

tried anointing my head with
rose water from last week's full moon,
but felt no shift inside my rib cage

I put you in a spell jar
and sealed it with wax from a black candle,
prayed to Goddess Hecate for help
to either bring you home
or banish you once and for all

but not this thing, not the in-between
where I hope with cupped hands
and I ask Hypnos for a good night's sleep

I just want to rid myself of your ghost—
I'll even give you two coins for the Boatman
if you'll just go

the truth is,
I finally know I am worth more
than your indecision

so stay if you'd like,

or go

if you cannot be what I need

CAN'T A GIRL JUST EAT A PINT OF ICE CREAM WHEN SHE'S SAD?

In the throes of a breakup, I should be able to pull a pint of Ben & Jerry's Americone Dream from the freezer box. (Because America, right?) A spoon from the drawer. My favorite red wine in a coffee mug. And sit in the center of my bed. 2005's *Pride & Prejudice* on the television so I can cry when Elizabeth Bennet cries. Softly rock my heartache to sleep and begin the healing process. No one telling me not to eat my feelings. No one telling me maybe I've let myself go. No guilt trip about empty calories. Just be left alone to feel everything. Given permission to write a poem about heartbreak and nothing else.

SPEAK IT INTO EXISTENCE

I ring the bell at my altar three times,
ignite the wick of a pale pink candle,
add rose petals and Himalayan salt
to my bowl

I write
I AM BEAUTIFUL
I AM BEAUTIFUL
I AM BEAUTIFUL

on a sage leaf in big, bold letters and add it,
bury it in cinnamon,
set it on fire

wish
and wait

HALFWAY THERE

there's a moment along your travels,
a point in time when you stop
to look at how far you've come

you check the soles of your shoes
and how much trail mix you have left,
pull out the map to trace it with your finger

halfway—
you're halfway there

and even though everyone tells you
it's not about the destination,
feeds you the line how it's
about the journey,
tells you not to look back,

we are fascinatingly curious creatures,
hell-bent on breaking rules
and acting like we wouldn't
sign our soul away for a little
divine intervention skewed our way

it's called *the collective pretend*

but I digress

halfway—
you're halfway home

SOMEDAY

I think someday I'd like to cradle myself,
wrap my arms around this body I call home,
flatten palms against my milky skin without
flinching, run fingertips over each curve,
commit them to memory—a new memory—
one in which I don't cringe

someday

I think someday I'd like to hug my thighs,
watch my stretch marks glisten, look at them
without contempt in my heart, understand
that growth of any kind doesn't come
without scars. I should like to not hate
my cellulite

someday

I think someday I'd like to love all of me,
every bone in my body, every tightening muscle,
all the fat, every imperfection from my too-small ears
to my precarious nose, and even my twisted tongue
that often feeds me lies about what I see in the mirror

someday

maybe today isn't that day,
maybe it won't be tomorrow either,
but I feel a swelling in my chest, a heart aching
for peace, and I know—I know someday
is coming soon

TRYING TO GET A MEDICAL DIAGNOSIS AS A FAT PERSON

for Naroba from Oklahoma

is as promising as winning the lottery
when you didn't even buy a ticket

you're sick because you're fat,
you're tired because you're fat,
you're throwing up because you're fat

you're fat because you eat too much,
you're fat because you don't exercise enough,
you're fat because you aren't trying

nothing is wrong with you,
nothing can help you,
nothing matters because you're fat

my pleas for help fall on the deaf ears
of people who took an oath to help,
and I'm dismissed as though my fat body
is less worthy of their healing hands

if you're fat, everything that's wrong with you
is because you're fat

I begged,
please tell me how my body is betraying me

I don't remember the exact moment I slipped
into the darkness but I remember the moment
I felt a concerned hand on my shoulder,

lifting me out for the very first time

there's a strange kind of relief when they
tell you you're not crazy

how I wept
when I finally heard the words
a *real* diagnosis

how I wept
when I finally knew
I was going to be okay

PERMISSION

if you want to turn a boy to stone
(and I say boy because no man would),
unpack your bags in front of him,
pull out all your pain and set it on the front lawn,
unwrinkle the mess of diary pages
where you recount your heartaches one by one,
roll up your sleeves and show him
the scars you've collected in your yesterdays

take off your makeup,
get naked,
trace your stretch marks,
point out your cellulite,
peel back every layer

let him see the peach pit of who you are
under the flesh,
hiding behind the bone,
be unapologetic

and if . . .
if he stays—not as a pile of ash,
not looking for the exit sign—

if he stays and takes you by the hand
and brushes your hair behind your ear,
if he asks you where it hurts,

it's okay to cry,

and it's okay to tell him

A RESPONSE TO THE MAN WHO TOLD ME HE WOULD TOTALLY FUCK ME IF I WAS SKINNIER

my body has value because it exists in this life
whether you want to fuck it or not

you are not the maker or breaker of me

besides,
who said I'd let you?

THE NORTH STAR

I pressed the North Star to my chest
but it did not take me home—
people say the sky is falling,
but they're liars

I can feel it ripping me open
from the inside, and anyone
who's ever written about the beauty
of the Universe in them has never
had their lungs swallowed up
by a black hole

inside me is a vast expanse and you can
romanticize it if you want,
but the truth is I spend most nights
trying to throw up the sickled moon
caught in my throat

when I was a child, they told me
I could be anything I wanted—
what they meant was I would grow up
to be an astronaut light years away
from a place to call home
and it would be my job to find it

I pressed the North Star to my chest
and it did not take me home

but I am still trying to get there

even though
you turned out to be
a complete and total
cliché of an asshole,
I still appreciate
your relentless insistence
that I'm beautiful

FETISH

past lovers would have me believe
my body was only an instrument
for their pleasure

I love a thick girl

they'd dig their hands into me,
claw their way around as if
they were hoping to find something else,
something more

more cushion for the pushin'

it's a difficult thing to unlearn,
existing only for others

I'll admit I struggle with it even now,
even as I swim deep through my truth,
even in knowing I am so much more
than what they branded me

thick thighs save lives

they make jokes out of our bodies,
make us a fetish they need to fulfill,
call us what they need to in order
to make us more palatable

but I'll never stop fighting
for what I know I deserve

real love

and neither should you

HANDLE WITH CARE

unravel me
the way
you would
a spool
of lace,

careful
not to
split me at
the edges

in more ways
than my
hardened heart
cares to
admit,
I am
delicate

and I need
someone
to help me
tell my story

SELF-SABOTAGE

people treat you the way you let them—
those were his words

and that was probably the most painful truth
that ever came charging through my insides,
settling like black tar in the bottom of my lungs

the hardest truths are often the ones
that need to be spoken loudest,
that need to be heard the most

I held on to his last few words
as I gathered the strength to let him go

I don't think either of us knew
he would be his own demise

we are always at war with the truths
we keep locked inside, which slowly try
to make their way into the light

lay down your sword

open the gates

let them come

you will be scarred and beaten,
but they will no longer be
crushing your windpipe

breathe

you're going to be just fine

SELF-PRESERVATION

throw out all the old bath towels he ever used,
and buy new soap because the old kind will
always smell like him

wrap your mattress in new sheets
and pile too many pillows on the
empty side of the bed

stop watching the shows you watched together,
and refrain from going to that bar down the street
where you both got drunk and made out

unframe the perfectly angled photographs,
throw out the calorie charts he made you
keep on the fridge

delete phone numbers, let him keep the kitchen table
so you can't see the ghost of him sitting across
from you as you eat plain oatmeal

you cannot unmeet him,
but you can unknow him,
you can unlearn his damage

this is not getting over him—
this is just what self-preservation looks like

SMALL VICTORIES

take notice of the first time
you look in the mirror
and it doesn't make you cringe,
doesn't make you want to shatter it

remember the time you tried
on a new outfit and really liked it,
how it hugged you just right,
the way you smiled only for yourself

hold on to the first time
you don't count calories,
or pull at your clothes,
or stare at the floor
as you walk past a strange man

each of those moments
is a victory

your victory

and it only gets easier from here

THE GIRL IN THE MIRROR

she doesn't know it yet—
and quite frankly neither do you—
but that girl in the mirror is going
to save you

the two of you spend most days
up in arms with one another,
hoping the other will surrender—
trust me, I know

she's a stubborn one,
that girl in the mirror

but then again, so are you,
so are we all

you should get to know her again,
just as I have

wouldn't it be lovely if you were
friends again one day?

that's all we can really ask for,
isn't it?

THE SUN

I'm sitting outside in my backyard,
warm light licking at my exposed skin,
and this is the sort of beautiful day
where you should find yourself happy

though I think *I will be happy one day*
if that's any consolation

the sun is perfect for things
like spurring photosynthesis,
drying tears,
and bringing tomorrow

THE WILD IN ME

I remember being uncorrupted—
virgin petals, untamed and uncut hips,
thorns still intact

it's the picture of myself
I'm working every day to reclaim

I've missed the wild in me,
but it's coming home, it's almost here,
and I've already promised myself
to never let another pluck my petals
or cut off my thorns
and leave me defenseless

my wild is coming back to me,
and this time
I'm ready to own it

A SPELL FOR THE HEALING

WELCOME HOME, I'M SURE YOU'VE MISSED BEING HERE

I know it can be easy to find yourself so far away
that you can't see the porch light anymore
this is advanced magic,
only the truly tried and tested make it here

let's cut a fresh orange open, leave the peel,
to fill you with insight,
and add it to lemon balm for peace
rue is quite powerful so take caution,
but it'll help keep the darkness at bay

sprinkle black pepper over all of it,
along with the light you found within yourself

take eight to ten beautiful memories
and use thyme to protect them

remember the lavender

repeat three times:
my body is beautiful and I am deserving of love,
my soul is magic and I am in love with myself

anoint your skin all over,
especially the pulse points and behind your ears
keep it on your bedside table and use it
anytime you feel the least bit worried
you'll slip outside of the light again*

no one is perfect, it will probably happen from time to time,
but remember the strength you have within yourself and you'll be fine

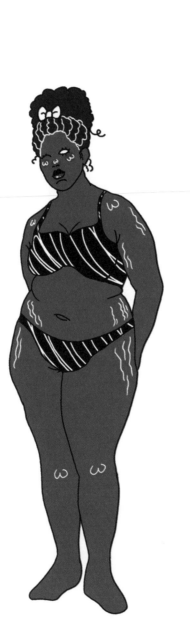

somewhere along the way
I forgot I am a goddess
and began holding myself captive

but not anymore

but never again

DECRIMINALIZE THE FAT BODY

let no man put us to death
for a crime we didn't commit,
for an apology we do not owe

uncuff us from the hospital bed—
we don't need a sedative,
and we will not piss in a cup for you

pull our bodies from the morgue
because this is not an autopsy,
you will not cut us open today

our bodies carry us,
have carried us this far,
and we do not need your handout

no man will judge us—
you are not the jury,
not the executioner

my body will never forgive me
if I let you find it guilty
for existing

AN OPEN CASKET

I make a gift of dried nettle,
shove it into wanting palms,
place my favorite raw calcite
next to my posed elbow,
weave mint into my hair,
say goodbye to this version of myself

I hardly recognize her

SPACE

I take up space

       and when I say I take up space

I don't mean

the number on the scale

or the one written inside my jeans

or the scoring system of my hotness

       I mean

       I am vehement

       I am robust

       I am more

I pour into a room
       and engulf you
           in everything I am

I mean I cannot be
       cut or folded down
           into something easier
              for you to swallow

OPEN SEASON
for K Leigh from Tennessee

you take shots at me
so often, in fact,
I spend most nights
cleaning buckshot
from between my teeth

you sow unease between
me and the food on my plate
each time you weigh me
with your invisible scales

but I will not be fooled by you,
you've never concerned yourself
with balance

judgment pours from your mouth
like a hot spring, the kind that would
slowly boil me to death
if I sat still long enough

hear me now,
hear this,
a declaration

I am no one's prey,
my body will not be
mounted to your wall,
you cannot take me to market

I am the hunter,
not the hunted

tell me I'm beautiful
through every season of my life

or never

NO PART OF ME WILL BE DENIED

the first time I touched another woman,
her smooth skin beneath my fingertips,
the silhouette of her body
plump and full, the same as my own,
it left a mark deep within me

something beautiful,
as natural as breathing

I felt a shift within myself
and never looked back,
never gave a second thought
to what's right or wrong,

because love is right,
all love

and
I will not deny
my mind
my body
my heart
anything
anymore

ALARM CLOCK

I no longer dream about being what you want,
no longer want to mold myself into what you need

I wasn't meant to fit, I've made peace with that—
I can't be for everyone, love

I am nothing if I'm so universal that I have
no unique parts

I am nothing if I lose myself inside the expectations
of everyone else

when my alarm sounds, I don't wish to recoil and hide

for once, morning feels like a place I can call home

I light a candle for every apology
I whisper to myself
under the Goddess Moon

I am so sorry I have betrayed you

I am so sorry I have betrayed myself

I WILL FIGHT

my body is mine
to love
to give
to govern

and I will fight
tooth and nail

I will scratch
I will bite
I will howl

at the Goddess Moon

to the death
to the death

I will fight
for my body
for my life

THE VIOLENT JOURNEY TO WOMANHOOD

I thought becoming a woman was a pretty thing—
I thought you woke up suddenly one day,
breasts bloomed, no longer a flat and hollow cage

I thought you woke up suddenly one day
not all knees and elbows, no longer half-tomboy,
trading in white cotton panties with days
of the week printed on them for lace thongs, black

I thought becoming a woman was gentle,
sophisticated, but I was wrong

no one tells you about the aches,
the growing pains as tectonic plates shift,
give way to mammary, give way
to more breast and less bone

no one tells you about the awkward walk
down the school hallway to ask for what is
formally known as a feminine hygiene product
*(even though many still call it a luxury item and
I would like to know when the fuck this became
a luxury),* your Tuesday panties dripping red
(your mother will never get them clean),
and all your weeks are ruined

I thought becoming a woman was beautiful
but it's strange and awkward, your body
collapsing in on itself, rebuilding itself
into something you don't recognize,
your best guy friend looking at you differently,
his voice cracking,

your body cracking

I thought becoming a woman was beautiful
but it emerges violently, is met with violence,
your body a vessel which might someday carry life
(but it's okay if it never does),
sexualized from the start, shamed for being
too sexy
or too fat
or too thin
or too (insert another adjective)

and aren't you tired yet?

be kind to your body,
woman, Goddess,
be kind because
others may not

and it is your home

BY ANY OTHER NAME

there are many names
I call myself
and many more
I have been given
by others

I am mother
I am sister
I am daughter
I am artist
I am manager
I am bitch
I am writer
I am poet
I am lover
I am cunt
I am bisexual
I am survivor
I am baby
I am victim
I am single
I am fat
I am woman
I am woman
I am woman

and I am fierce

and you are not allowed
to use any of these names
against me

JUST TEN POUNDS

for Anonymous in Washington

I held my grandmother's paper hand,
listening to eighty years of wisdom,
only for her to tell me about the
ten pounds still eluding her,
the ten pounds she still wanted
to leave behind

and it broke my heart to think
about all she's seen and felt
and heard and lived through,
but this was the demon
she was still battling,
the skeleton she hadn't yet
dismantled

and in this, more wisdom,
another lesson she unknowingly
taught

because when I'm gray-haired,
holding my granddaughter's hand
and looking back on my life,
I refuse to feel the sting
of darkness squatting inside a place
I only want to fill with love

I refuse to let my body
be anything less than sunlight

I CAN BE TWO THINGS

I am full moon round,
tired and bright,
tired some more

this world tells me
I can't be more than this,
more than one thing

but I am burning
orange-yellow leaves
from the great oak

in my backyard,
falling and floating,
falling some more

I tell them I will be
as many things as
my body will let me,

as many things
as my soul
will make me

I tell them
I can shoulder it,
I can be enough

in this life and the next,
to be sky and earth,
weightless and grounded

you can tell them
you are strong enough too
you can tell them

your bones will carry it
and if you don't believe
you can, do it anyway

you will surprise yourself,
this I know,
this I promise

I don't know what version of me you fell in love with

but I know I dislike the one I became underneath your thumb,

how she cowered and bowed and hoped—

if that's the woman you're looking for,

she doesn't exist here anymore

WHEN MY MIND IS CHAOS, I GO SHOE SHOPPING

The perfectly predictable promised fit of a pair of shoes means I don't have to look at myself in the mirror, don't have to smooth and tuck and suck in, and don't have to turn red and hot under the fluorescent lights of the dressing room. It means I won't feel bad when I go to dinner later and think about the disappointment of my shopping trip, causing me to order a side salad and water. It means I can look down at my feet adorned in beautiful brand-new shoes and feel a touch of pride instead of disdain for one fleeting moment of my day.

QUEEN OF THE WOLVES

I have no intention
of kneeling to a man
who isn't willing
to kneel to me

so if he wants to be a wolf,
I'll let him be a wolf—
he can gnash and claw,
bite and howl

I'll remind him from time to time
that I eat wolves for breakfast,
bones and all,
and better men have been
on their knees for me,
begging

Queen of the Wolves,
he calls me

you have to be savage
to tame one,
but don't misunderstand me

this has never been
about their obedience,
only their willingness
to give what they expect

so if he wants me
to be a wolf too,
I'll be a wolf—

I'll bite and howl,
gnash and claw

a beast will always want
to love a queen

so I am a queen, waiting

TINDER MOMENTS #3

he told me I was pretty

and I told him to tell me something I didn't know

BEAST IN MY HEAD
for Erica from California

I call it anxiety,
I call it a self-discomfort—
it's the beast in my head
I fight against

the photo of me
thirty pounds lighter,
wearing a dress I no longer own,
is it false advertising?
does it paint me a liar?

and while the fear
I'll never be good enough
continues to override
all the other thoughts,
I know someday
I'll be strong enough
to take a new photo,
to buy a new dress,
to embrace the new
curves of my body,
and I'll be good enough

I'll be me

maybe I don't wake up every morning
and love myself wholly and completely as I am,
that much I will confess

but let's be reasonable and humble—
no one really does that every single day without fail,
this I know to be true

because it's not about what we feel when we rise,
but how we face each day in spite of it,
and how we return to ourselves each night

BURN IT DOWN

recoil, pull inward, back up

make them wonder
where you've gone,
what you're doing,
why you're not
at their beck and call

make them miss you,
your light, the warmth
of your fire,
your smooth skin they use
for their pleasure

make them wish they
hadn't smothered you,
doused you in water,
reduced you to soot

after you dry out
in the yellow sun,
after they welcome
you back,
after you relight yourself
(because you will relight yourself)

burn it down,
burn it all down—
make them sorry

does the doctor tell you

that all your anxiety will disappear

if you lose weight,

or is it just me?

EAT THE COOKIE

don't eat the cookie and do extra sit-ups
don't eat the cookie and skip a meal
don't eat the cookie in hiding
don't eat the cookie in shame
don't eat the cookie and cry

just eat the damn cookie

and smile

you will be in your own skin
longer than you will be anywhere else

make it more than a battleground of insecurities,
more than a personal game of capture the self-love flag

make it a place where you let deserving lovers rest,
a place for deep belly laughs and cleansing cries

make it a home there in your skin,
and let its inherent mystery bewilder onlookers

dare to be amazed with yourself

you don't have to love yourself all day

you don't even have to love yourself most of the day
(although those things are the goal)

you just have to love yourself enough to wake up and face the day
(whatever it may bring)

WHEN IT IS QUIET

I like the silent moments
nestled between the ones
too loud to hear myself think,
moments so quiet I would swear
I was floating somewhere
near Venus

when everything is stone silent
enough to hear my own heart beating,
I close my eyes, slow my breathing,
and remember,

I am still whole

all by myself

my heart beats for me

YOU DON'T LIKE ME

because I fill the room,
because I take up too much space,
because I am so much bigger than you

but I'm not talking about the flesh covering my bones
or how it signals to you not to respect me

what I mean is,
I've exhumed my confidence from the rubble,
wear my stretch marks like chain mail,
am worth more than my weight in gold
(and that's a lot of gold)

what I mean is,
where once I was hollow hands making myself fit around you,
I am now something divine, something to be worshiped

what I mean is,
I am thick, round, soft edges, smooth, beautiful

you don't like me and that's alright,
there's no accounting for taste,
and I'm sweet on your tongue
like butter, cinnamon-swirled dough

no,
you cannot have a taste
      no,
       I am not a doormat
          no,
            you are not welcome here

FAT GIRLS

they tell me
fat girls cannot be graceful
they tell me
fat girls cannot be beautiful
they tell me
fat girls are only a fetish,
only a phase,
only for one night

they tell me
he will never take me home to meet his mom
or his friends, that he will never show me off with pride

they tell me
he carries shame around when he holds my hand

stupid fat girl, they say,
you cannot be loved

I could say many things,
could shout many harsh words
but none of it matters

instead I tell them about my lover's slender hip bones
cradled by my thick thighs,
how his mother loves me as much as he loves me

I tell them *he loves me*
and I know it
and I can feel it

all over *my big,*
beautiful body

A MANTRA FOR LIVING

I have wept and will weep again
but not for my body, not for my home

I have hurt and will hurt again
but not for my skin, not for my bones

I will love me as I have loved lovers,
I will forgive myself as I have forgiven blood,

and I will hold myself in the same light
in which the sun holds the moon

because I am the only thing that is forever

I am a fat girl

I am valid

I am magic

if you made it here, that's amazing,
but you're not done, not even close

unfortunately loving yourself is
a rinse-and-repeat process

a process,
not a destination

so start from the beginning again
if you must

start from the beginning
and I'll see you here again

A NOTE FROM THE AUTHOR

My dear, sweet reader—if you picked this collection up, chances are you've felt shame. Shame for your fat body because society made it clear that fat = disgusting. And I'm sorry they did that to you.

I'm sorry for every time someone called you fat, laughed in your face, called you names under their breath, or belittled you in some way simply for existing. I'm sorry you feel like no one understands. Because I do. And that's why I wrote this collection.

Too often, we shoulder it all, hold on to every insult hurled our way. And as if that weren't enough, we take them back out on quiet nights when our thoughts are too loud to ignore and use them as reasons to hate ourselves, reasons to starve ourselves, to consider plastic surgery or insane exercise routines. In turn, we develop terrible relationships with fitness and food.

I've been there so many times myself. So if you take anything away from this collection, let it be this—you are so much more than a fat girl. You are beautiful, kind, smart, and strong. You have talents. You have a voice. Not the one inside you that reminds you what others have said about you in the past. You have a big fat set of lungs and you can scream if you want.

You have a big fat heart and you can love yourself and sometimes it will feel like an act of rebellion.

The point is, I love you. And loving yourself is not a destination always out of reach. It's a never-ending journey with highs and lows, curved roads, and rickety bridges. It's sunny days and stormy nights. Sometimes you'll go so far in a single day, you don't recognize your surroundings. And some days you'll need to rest your aching feet. That's okay.

Keep going. Never stop trying. You can do this.

ACKNOWLEDGMENTS

First and foremost, I want to thank Michelle Halket at Central Avenue for giving me this amazing opportunity and platform to share my work with the world. Thank you for seeing something special in me and taking a chance. Thank you to the rest of the team at Central Avenue, Beau, Jessica, and Molly, for helping me make this collection the best it could be.

Thank you to my daughter, Kali, who I had the honor of hiring to do all of the beautiful illustrations you see inside this book. I'm so proud you're my daughter. You can be anything you want to be. And to my other children, Mattie and Kaden, thank you for being an inspiration to me every single day. I love you all so much.

To Brittany, my little sister, who's my biggest fan and best friend. Thank you for always being the best cheerleader. I love you.

My mother, Kim, and sister Angela, who have both passed on—thank you for my roots, for shaping me, for being by my side growing up. I love you and miss you both more than words can express.

Thank you to my partner, Chris. You've believed in me and my talent since the very first day we met. You've encouraged, supported, and loved me through thick and thin. I love you, babe.

To all the women who inspire me, sustain me, and challenge me from by my side and from afar—Jen R., Courtney W., Cynthia R., Kayleigh B., Shannon O., Alix K., Trista M., Tarryn F., Colleen H., Trish A., and so many more—thank you for everything you do.

Thank you to all those who submitted your stories to me and entrusted me with your secrets and insecurities. I hope you can move forward in confidence and love for yourself and your body.

USA Today Bestselling Author Kat Savage is a mother
first, and spends the rest of her time penning novels,
scrawling poetry, and designing book covers. As a major
advocate for body positivity, self-love, and eradicating
fatphobia, she often shares many of her own raw truths
and lessons she learned the hard way in hopes of helping
the next goddess find their inner strength.
If she's not writing or working, you can find her playing
with her dogs, reading, or hanging out on Instagram.

@kat.savage